Abundance of the Heart

BOB *and* **EMILIE BARNES**

Paintings by Carolyn Shores Wright

HARVEST HOUSE PUBLISHERS
Eugene, Oregon

Abundance of the Heart

Text Copyright © 2000 Harvest House Publishers
Eugene, Oregon 97402

Library of Congress Cataloging–in–Publication Data
Barnes, Bob, 1933-
    Abundance of the heart / Bob and Emilie Barnes ; paintings by Carolyn Shores Wright.
        p.   cm.
    ISBN 0-7369-0260-0
    1. Fruit of the Spirit Prayer–books and devotions—English.
  I. Barnes, Emilie. II. Title.
  BV4501.2.B382854   2000
  234' .13—dc21

                                        99-37261
                                            CIP

All works of art reproduced in this book are copyrighted by Carolyn Shores Wright and are reproduced under license from © Arts Uniq'®, Inc., Cookeville, TN. For information regarding art prints featured in this book, please contact:

    Arts Uniq'
    P.O. Box 3085
    Cookeville, TN 38502
    800-223-5020

Design and production by Garborg Design Works, Minneapolis, Minnesota

Harvest House Publishers has made every effort to trace the ownership of all poems and quotes. In the event of a question arising from the use of a poem or quote, we regret any error made and will be pleased to make the necessary correction in future editions of this book.

Unless otherwise indicated, Scripture quotations are taken from the New American Standard Bible, © 1960, 1962, 1963, 1968, 1971, 1972, 1973, 1975, 1977 by The Lockman Foundation. Used by permission. Scriptures marked NIV are from the Holy Bible, New International Version®, Copyright © 1973, 1978, 1984 by the International Bible Society.

Printed in the United States of America.

00 01 02 03 04 05 06 07 08 09 / IP / 10 9 8 7 6 5 4 3 2 1

This book is dedicated to the many Christian
friends who have shown me

Love 🍎 Joy 🍎 Peace 🍎
Patience 🍎 Kindness 🍎 Goodness 🍎
Gentleness 🍎 Self-Control

during my recent illness. All of your cards, letters, gifts,
phone calls, e-mails, and prayers have blessed my life.
You have been God's expression to me that "all's well."
Your caring and concern have beautifully reflected the
fruit of the Spirit—love in action.

Thank you for sharing your gifts with me. I only
trust that I can be as giving to those around me who
need a touch of the fruit.

May you continue to reach out and give people who
are in need that special gift we have as children of God.

Nine Beautiful Words

As I have grown in my Christian walk, I have discovered that many things are at work in my life during any given time. As a sixteen-year-old Jewish girl who had recently accepted Jesus as my Messiah, I became aware of these wonderful things—good overcoming evil, forgiveness triumphing over sin, life eclipsing death, and light outshining darkness. I saw more clearly the positive actions of others and their rewarding consequences.

I didn't yet have a deep understanding of my faith, but I did know that I wanted to have an eternal impact on the lives of the people I met. After I heard the "good news," I eagerly responded, "Now what, Lord?" But of course all my questions were not answered right away. Now, after forty-five years of studying the Scriptures, I have begun to realize what I was searching for in my early life as a believer. I wanted to know how to take God's Word and live it out in my everyday actions. I wanted the fruit of the Spirit to be at work in my day-to-day life.

What is the fruit of the Spirit? According to Galatians 5:22,23, "...the fruit of the Spirit is love, joy, peace, patience, kindness, goodness, faithfulness, gentleness, and self-control." These are all very good things for a Christian to exhibit in her life!

As I read this verse again and again over the years, I have tended to hurriedly skim over each descriptive trait without seeking out in-depth what the Scripture has to say about each one. However, once I look at these traits closely, I see exactly what I want my life to reflect as a follower of Jesus. I consider these nine magnificent words to be the "grace" words of the Christian life.

If each of us could make these words the spiritual goals for our lives, we could have an incredible influence upon the world around us. Our churches would be overflowing with people as we lovingly attend to the needs of the lost. And the whole world would be lifted up by the sweet fragrance of forgiveness and acceptance.

As you read through my reflections and the thoughts of others about each of these nine important qualities, I pray that you will become aware of the power of each word and grasp why Paul used these particular terms to illustrate the goodness of the gospel.

My hope is for you to discover how to live out your Christian faith in a meaningful way that has a healing effect on a hurting world.

May the Holy Spirit empower you to reflect love, joy, peace, patience, kindness, goodness, faithfulness, gentleness, and self-control in your life, each and every day.

Blessings,

Emilie Barnes

Contents

CHAPTER ONE

Love

But now abide faith, hope, love, these three: but the greatest of these is love.

1 CORINTHIANS 13:13

All of us spend a good part of our lives earnestly searching for the most rewarding feeling of all—something called love. As tiny babies, we look to those around us to give us love. Later on in life, we read books and magazines, attend seminars and workshops, and have long conversations with others, attempting to improve our understanding of love. And despite our best efforts, we still have a hard time defining love. So what is this sought-after feeling? According to Scripture, it's much more than just a fleeting emotion. Instead, love is a decision that we consciously make, and it's shown in how we treat other people. When we love

them, we choose to do what is best for them. The ultimate example of this kind of love is found in the primary love that God has for us. "For God so loved the world, that He gave His only begotten Son, that whosoever believes in Him should not perish, but have eternal life" (John 3:16).

Now that's love! In spite of our not always choosing to do things His way, God gave us His only Son so that we might be forgiven and delight in His everlasting caring. When we are able to capture the magnitude of His love, we gain an immense understanding of what love is all about. And we gradually discover that He has placed in us a capacity to love others far beyond what we could ever imagine. Through this we begin to love God, love ourselves, and love others. In fact, this becomes our main mission in life. This kind of love—agape love, the highest expression of love— can conquer all. It comes directly from heaven, and when it enters our hearts, we all are truly blessed with its rewards!

And you shall love the LORD your God with all your heart and with all your soul and with all your might.

DEUTERONOMY 6:5

There is a substitute for criticism. It's called love. Love heals. Love protects.

Love builds up. And more change occurs with love than with criticism.

H. NORMAN WRIGHT

Beloved, let us love one

Many waters cannot quench love, nor will rivers overflow it.

SONG OF SOLOMON 8:7

It is love in old age, no longer blind, that is true love. For love's highest intensity doesn't necessarily mean its highest quality. Glamour and jealousy are gone; and the ardent caress, no longer needed, is valueless compared to the reassuring touch of a trembling hand. Passersby commonly see little beauty in the embrace of young lovers on a park bench, but the understanding smile of an old wife to her husband is one of the loveliest things in the world.

BOOTH TARKINGTON

There is no fear in love; but perfect love casts out fear.
1 JOHN 4:18

another, for love is from God.
1 JOHN 4:7

Little children let us not love

with word or with tongue,

but in deed and truth.
1 JOHN 3:18

Love is a fruit in season at all times, and within
reach of every hand. Anyone may gather it and
no limit is set. Everyone can reach
this love through meditation,
spirit of prayer, and
sacrifice, by an
intense inner life.
MOTHER TERESA

11

Love cannot be forced, love cannot be coaxed and teased. It comes out of Heaven unasked and unsought.

PEARL BUCK

A Child Learns About Love

I remember the morning that I first asked the meaning of the word "love." This was before I knew many words. I had found a few early violets in the garden and brought them to my teacher. She tried to kiss me; but at that time I did not like to have anyone kiss me except my mother. Miss Sullivan put her arm gently round me and spelled into my hand, "I love Helen."

"What is love?" I asked.

She drew me closer to her and said, "It is here," pointing to my heart....Her words puzzled me very much because I did not then understand anything unless I touched it.

I smelled the violets in her hand and asked, half in words, half in signs, a question which meant, "Is love the sweetness of flowers?"

"No," said my teacher.

Again I thought. The warm sun was shining on us.

"Is this not love?" I asked, pointing in the direction from which the heat came....

A day or two afterward...the sun had been under a cloud all day, and there had

Familiar acts are beautiful through love.

PERCY BYSSHE SHELLEY

12

been brief showers, but suddenly the sun broke forth in all its southern splendor. Again I asked my teacher, "Is this not love?"

"Love is something like the clouds that were in the sky before the sun came out," she replied. Then in simpler words than these, which at that time I could not have understood, she explained: "You cannot touch the clouds, you know; but you feel the rain and know how glad the flowers and the thirsty earth are to have it after a hot day. You cannot touch love either; but you feel the sweetness

The God of love my Shepherd is,
And He that doth me feed,
While He is mine, and I am His,
What can I want or need?
GEORGE HERBERT

We love, because He first loved us.
1 JOHN 4:19

that it pours into everything. Without love you would not be happy or want to play."

The beautiful truth burst upon my mind—I felt that these were invisible lines stretched between my spirit and the spirits of others.

HELEN KELLER

Love sought is good, but giv'n unsought is better.

SHAKESPEARE

Love is patient, love is kind, and is not jealous; love does not brag, and is not arrogant, does not act unbecomingly; it does not seek its own, is not provoked, does not take into account a wrong suffered, does not rejoice in unrighteousness, but rejoices with the truth; bears all things, hopes all things, endures all things. Love never fails.

1 CORINTHIANS 13:4-8

The best portion of a good man's life, his little, nameless, unremembered acts of kindness and love.

WILLIAM WORDSWORTH

Love is more than gold

So let us love, dear Love, like as we ought,
Love is the lesson which the Lord us taught.

EDMUND SPENSER

14

Love conquers all things:
let us too give in to Love.
VIRGIL

O God, who hast prepared for them that love thee such good
things as pass man's understanding; pour into our hearts such
love toward thee, that we, loving thee above all things, may
obtain thy promises, which exceed all that we can desire.
THE BOOK OF COMMON PRAYER

or great riches.
JOHN LYDGATE

Let those love now, who never lov'd before:
Let those who always lov'd, now love the more.
LATIN PROVERB

Prayer

Father God, as I look to You as the
supreme example of what love is, I feel so
inadequate to reflect the agape love that You
show each and every one of Your children.
Yet I am inspired by Your standard. I know
that You are love, and I want my life to
reflect to those around me
Your sense of love for all
people. After all, it was You
who sent Your only Son to
come to earth, live as a
man, and die on the cross
for the atonement of all our sins so that
with His resurrection we might join You in
heaven for eternity. Please continue to
remind me when I need to show Your love
to someone else so that the world can see
You through my life. Amen.

And this I pray,
that your love may
abound still more
and more.
PHILIPPIANS 1:9

CHAPTER TWO

Joy

A joyful heart is good medicine.

PROVERBS 17:22

Many times we expect the fruit of joy to bring us unlimited happiness and fun times. Yet when we read the Scriptures, we are encouraged to reflect on what it really means to experience joy and to have a joyful heart. Happiness and fun are good in themselves, but they come and go with circumstances. Joy, however, is felt beyond our circumstances. Joy can be experienced even when times are difficult.

Joy is an attitude we have toward life's experiences. It is a treasure of the heart, a comforting knowing of God's intimate presence. As we view the events of our life, we can choose to be resentful toward God for letting certain things happen to us or

Find joy in simplicity, self-respect, and indifference to what lies between virtue and vice. Love the human race. Follow the divine.

MARCUS AURELIUS

we can choose an attitude of gratitude and a commitment to joy. Joy is our best choice. We have joy when we are serving God and doing what He wants for our lives. We have joy when we learn to take our circumstances and the ups and downs of life in stride and use all situations to bring glory to God. We lighten our load in life and draw others to us by having a joyful heart. When we have joy in the Lord, we begin to see life from God's point of view, and we realize that things have never looked so beautiful, so peaceful, so amazing. The joy of the Lord is our strength!

These things I have spoken to you, that My joy may be in you, and that your joy may be full.

JOHN 15:11

17

This is the true joy in life, the

being used for a purpose recognized

by yourself as a mighty one.

GEORGE BERNARD SHAW

Behold, how good and joyful a thing it is

for brethren, to dwell together in unity!

THE BOOK OF COMMON PRAYER

Rejoice in the Lord

Rejoice always; pray without ceasing; in everything give thanks; for this is God's will for you in Christ Jesus.

1 THESSALONIANS 5:16-18

The joy of the LORD is your strength.

NEHEMIAH 8:10

Joyful, joyful, we adore Thee,

God of glory, Lord of love;

Hearts unfold like flowers before Thee,

Opening to the sun above.

Melt the clouds of sin and sadness,

Drive the dark of doubt away;

Giver of immortal gladness,

Fill us with the light of day.

Shout joyfully to the LORD, all the earth. Serve the LORD
with gladness; come before Him with joyful singing.

PSALM 100:1

always; again I will say, rejoice!

PHILIPPIANS 4:4

All Thy works with joy surround Thee,

Earth and heaven reflect Thy rays,

Stars and angels sing around Thee,

Center of unbroken praise.

Field and forest, vale and mountain,

Flowery meadow, flashing sea,

Chanting bird and flowing fountain,

Call us to rejoice in Thee.

Thou art giving and forgiving,

Ever blessing, ever blest,

Wellspring of the joy of living,

Ocean depth of happy rest!

Thou our Father, Christ our Brother,

All who live in love are Thine;

Teach us how to love each other,

Lift us to the joy divine.

HENRY VAN DYKE

Sing praises unto the Lord,
O ye saints of his; and
give thanks unto him for a
remembrance of his
holiness...heaviness may
endure for a night, but joy
cometh in the morning.

THE BOOK OF COMMON PRAYER

How good is man's life, the mere living! how fit to employ
All the heart and the soul and the senses, for ever in joy!

ROBERT BROWNING

A joyful heart makes

For to a person who is good in
His sight He has given wisdom
and knowledge and joy.

ECCLESIASTES 2:26

Shout joyfully to God, all the earth;
Sing the glory of His name.
Make His praise glorious.

PSALM 66:1,2

Let the rivers clap their hands; let the mountains sing together for joy.

PSALM 98:8

Make my joy complete by being of the same mind, maintaining the same love, united in spirit, intent on one purpose.

PHILIPPIANS 2:2

a cheerful face.

PROVERBS 15:13

But let all who take refuge in Thee be glad,

Let them ever sing for joy.

PSALM 5:11

Father God, You know that joy belongs next to love and that our entire being should reflect this great virtue. To me, joy is the beam of sunshine that shines in the believer's presence. Its rays reach out to the world through our sorrows and defeats, as well as in our jubilations and triumphs. Joy is the sunshine that is ever present for the child of God. Please help me to freely show how joyful I am at all times. Your Scripture is very clear when it says that we are to be "always rejoicing." I want to be known as a joyful person, one who reflects the positive side of *all* of life. The world is seeking out those of us who are authentic in our walk with You. Let me remember that joy is when there is nothing between Jesus and me. I thank You for reflecting the joy of my salvation. Amen.

CHAPTER THREE

Peace

The LORD will give strength to His people;
the LORD will bless His people with peace.

PSALM 29:11

Peace is something the whole world dreams of attaining. We see banners that call for peace. Peace symbols adorn buses, backpacks, and bumper stickers. Peace is pleaded for everywhere and in every language. There is even a "Beanie Baby" named Peace. Very few people in our world, in fact, do not wish for peace. And peace—lasting peace—is certainly what we all need. Peace, as defined by the fruit of the Spirit, is a Christian virtue of assured quietness of the soul. It is the opposite of our earthly struggles. It is best described as a "wellness between oneself and God."

The peace that God gives is built on the awareness that we all need a purpose and a cause for existing. As we mature in our spiritual nature and learn what this life is all about, we come to accept that only our heavenly Father can give us a calmness within ourselves. Once we realize this, we no longer must toss and turn trying to find answers to our struggle. We have reconciled with God through Jesus, His Son, that life indeed has meaning and that we are created in God's image. With this understanding, we can move on in life in a very meaningful way. We know the Alpha and the Omega. We are at peace with God, and we finally know who we are. We have inner peace of mind, soul, and spirit. There is a calmness to our presence. Our life reflects God's love and joy, and those around will be lifted up by our outward expression of this fruit of the Spirit.

Experience the perfect peace of
God in your life by realizing
anew that it is only obtained
through the presence of Christ in
our lives—He is our peace.
KENNETH W. OSBECK

Seek peace, and pursue it.

PSALM 34:14

O Lord my God, I thank Thee that Thou
hast brought this day to a close;
I thank Thee that Thou hast given me peace
in body and in soul.
Thy hand has been over me and has protected
and preserved me.

DIETRICH BONHOEFFER

Her ways are pleasant ways,

Finally, brethren, rejoice...be comforted,
be like minded, live in peace; and the
God of love and peace shall be with you.

2 CORINTHIANS 13:11

*I know not what I shall become: it seems to me that
peace of soul and repose of spirit descend on me, even
in sleep. To be without the sense of this peace, would
be affliction indeed.... I know not what God purposes
with me, or keeps me for; I am in a calm so great that
I fear naught. What can I fear, when I am with Him:
and with Him, in His Presence, I hold myself the
most I can. May all things praise Him. Amen.*

BROTHER LAWRENCE

24

Peace I leave with you; My peace I give to you; not as the world gives, do I give to you. Let not your heart be troubled; nor let it be fearful.

JOHN 14:27

God hath not promised

Skies always blue,

Flower-strewn pathways

All our lives through;

God hath not promised

Sun without rain,

Joy without sorrow,

Peace without pain.

and all her paths are peace.

PROVERBS 3:17

Peace is such a precious jewel that I would give anything for it but truth.

MATTHEW HENRY

But God hath promised

Strength for the day,

Rest for the labor,

Light for the way,

Grace for the trials,

Help from above,

Unfailing sympathy,

Undying love.

ANNIE JOHNSON FLINT

When peace, like a river, attendeth my way,

When sorrow like sea billows roll;

Whatever my lot, Thou hast taught me to say,

It is well, it is well with my soul.

HORATIO GATES SPAFFORD

25

Now may the Lord
of peace Himself
continually grant you
peace in every
circumstance.

2 THESSALONIANS 3:16

Thou wilt keep him in perfect peace
whose mind is stayed on Thee.
When the shadows come and darkness falls,
He giveth inward peace.
O, He is the only perfect resting place.
He giveth perfect peace!
Thou wilt keep him in perfect peace
whose mind is stayed on Thee.

VIVIAN KRETZ

A peace above all earthly dignities, a still and quiet conscience.

SHAKESPEARE

Blessed are the peacemakers, for t

*Ultimately, we have just one moral duty: to
reclaim large areas of peace in ourselves, more
and more peace, and to reflect it toward others.
And the more peace there is in us, the more
peace there will be in our troubled world.*

ETTY HILLESUM

Thou wilt keep him in perfect
peace, because he trusts in Thee.

ISAIAH 26:3

Love truth and peace.

ZECHARIAH 8:19

Like a river glorious is God's perfect peace,

Over all victorious in its bright increase;

Perfect, yet it floweth fuller every day,

Perfect, yet it groweth deeper all the way.

Stayed upon Jehovah, hearts are fully blest;

Finding, as He promised, perfect peace and rest.

FRANCES R. HAVERGAL

shall be called sons of God.

MATTHEW 5:9

Live in peace with one another.

1 THESSALONIANS 5:13

Father God, as I search for peace in my life, I realize that perfect peace only comes from knowing You. Because You are the Prince of Peace, You are also the giver of peace. I see around me so many people who seem restless in their souls, people who do not react with compassion to those whom they supposedly love. I thank You for producing the fruit of peace in the believer's life that is pleasing unto You. Keep me firmly attached to the vine, which gives us life, so that others may see the fruit of Your work in my life and give glory to God through Your Son Jesus Christ. I know that the fruit of peace will not develop overnight. May I continue to be willing and patient to develop my life along these precious virtues of the Christian life. Hold me close to You, so that You will mentor me in all things that are good. Amen.

27

Chapter Four

Patience

Rest in the Lord and wait patiently for Him.

PSALM 37:7

"Be still and know that I am God; I will be exalted among the nations, I will be exalted in the earth," declares Psalm 46:10 (NIV). This verse was the inspiration for Katharina von Schlege in 1752 to write the great hymn of the church "Be Still, My Soul." Reflecting on the fourth fruit of the Spirit, patience, Katharina penned, "Be still, my soul—the Lord is on my side! Bear patiently the cross of grief or pain. Leave to thy God to order and provide. In ev'ry change He faithful will remain. Be still, my

soul—thy best, thy heavenly Friend through thorny ways leads to a joyful end." And in Isaiah 40:31 the message remains faithful: "Those who wait for the Lord will gain new strength."

This waiting is not always easy for me. I am the kind of person who likes to take charge and accomplish things according to my own schedule. I must continually work at being patient, letting God still my soul and show me His plans. However, each time I pray for patience, I'm not always pleased with what He sends my way. In fact, I've often half-jokingly told friends that I'm going to stop praying for patience because God always sends me such challenges! Somehow, though, the Lord knows exactly what I need to quiet my soul to listen to His voice. And I can truthfully say that my patience has grown with time. God certainly knows how to "still the soul," and I am most content when I am resting within His tender arms, following things according to His perfect plan for my life.

Live neither in the past nor in the future, but let each day's work absorb your entire energies, and satisfy your wildest ambition.
WILLIAM OSLER

And let us not lose heart in doing good, for in due time we shall reap if we do not grow weary.

GALATIANS 6:9

God's road is all uphill, but do not tire, rejoice that we may still keep climbing higher.

ARTHUR GITERMAN

To live in the presence of great truths, to be dealing with eternal laws, to be led by permanent ideals—that is what keeps a man patient when the world ignores him, and calm and unspoiled when the world praises him.

FRANCIS G. PEABODY

And the seed in the good soil, these are the ones who have heard the word in an honest and good heart, and hold it fast, and bear fruit with perseverance.

LUKE 8:15

I waited patiently for and He inclined to me,

Lord, give me sympathy and sense and help me keep my courage high.
God, give me calm and confidence~and, please~a twinkle in my eye.

MARGARET BAILEY

I avoid looking forward or backward,
and try to keep looking upward.

CHARLOTTE BRONTE

Let nothing disturb thee

Let nothing frighten thee

Everything is changing

God alone is changeless

Patience attains the goal

One who has God lacks nothing

God alone fills all our needs.

ST. THERESA OF AVILA

the Lord;
and heard my cry.

PSALM 40:1

Our patience will

Consider it all joy, my brethren...knowing that the testing of your faith produces endurance and let endurance have its perfect result, that you may be perfect and complete, lacking in nothing.

JAMES 1:2-4

But if we hope for what we do not see, with perseverance we wait eagerly for it.

ROMANS 8:25

The hero is one who kindles a great light in the world, who sets up blazing torches in the dark street of life for men to see by. The saint is the man who walks through the dark paths of the world, himself a light.

FELIX ADLER

Now may the God who gives perseverance and encouragement grant you to be of the same with one another according to Christ Jesus.

ROMANS 15:5

achieve more than our force.

EDMUND BURKE

Let us run with endurance the race that is set before us.

HEBREWS 12:1

We give thanks to God always for all of you...constantly bearing in mind your work of faith and labor of love and steadfastness of hope in our LORD Jesus Christ in the presence of our God and Father.

1 THESSALONIANS 1:2,3

Father God, as I stand before You, I think of all the lessons of patience You have taught me. Patience has become the guardian of my faith. It is the preserver of my peace, it is the cherisher of my love, and it is the teacher of my humility. I have seen patience produce unity in my church, harmony in my family, and extended cheerfulness in my adversity. Patience has taught me to forgive those who have injured me and to be the first in asking forgiveness of those whom I have hurt. I thank You for working in my life this great trait called patience. It has certainly helped to make me more like You, which is what I wish to become. Amen.

33

CHAPTER FIVE

Kindness

Be kind to one another, tender-hearted, forgiving each other,
just as God in Christ also has forgiven you.

EPHESIANS 4:32

One of the best compliments we can give a friend is to tell her that she is a kind person. When we look at the biblical concept of this fruit, we see that kindness is a gentle or tender action that comes from a spirit of concern or compassion. A kind person goes out of her way to be nice to someone else. Kindness is reflected by speaking with an authentic caring for others, mindful of their needs. Kindness is very much an attitude of the heart. We learn very early in life how to be kind. With our children, we continually talk to them about this cherished virtue. And all through Scripture we are shown God's character as we discover His many attributes of kindness.

Each day we can lighten someone's load and bring them joy by treating them nicely. It's worth it to make others feel important and to be kind to the people we meet. Say, "Good morning," and "How are you?" Volunteer, "Let me help you with that load," or "I'd like to get that door for you." Even simply a bright smile paired with a genuine compliment are sure to convey kindness. Heartfelt words and helpful deeds will always ease another's day. And who among us would not like to have our load eased? May you be the blessing in someone else's life today.

He who is gracious to a poor man lends to the LORD, and He will repay him for his good deed.

PROVERBS 19:17

Lord, make me an instrument of Thy peace; where there is hatred, let me sow love; where there is injury, pardon; where there is doubt, faith; where there is despair, hope; where there is darkness, light; where there is sadness, joy.

ST. FRANCIS OF ASSISI

Good actions are the invisible hinges on the doors of heaven.

VICTOR HUGO

What is desirable

While we have opportunity, let us do good to all men, and especially to those who are of the household of the faith.

GALATIANS 6:10

She opens her mouth in wisdom and the teaching of kindness is on her tongue.

PROVERBS 31:26

"But a certain Samaritan, who was on a journey, came upon him; and when he saw him, he felt compassion, and came to him, and bandaged up his wounds, pouring oil and wine on them; and he put him on his own beast, and brought him to an inn, and took care of him. And on the next day he took out two denarii and gave them to the innkeeper and said, 'Take care of him; and whatever more you spend, when I return, I will repay you.' Which of these three do you think proved to be a neighbor to the man who fell into the robbers' hands?" And he said, "The one who showed mercy toward him." And Jesus said to him, "Go and do the same."

LUKE 10:33-37

Let all be harmonious, sympathetic, brotherly,

kindhearted, and humble in spirit.

1 PETER 3:8

in a man is his kindness.

PROVERBS 19:22

Do all the good you can,

By all the means you can,

In all the ways you can,

In all the places you can,

At all the times you can,

To all the people you can,

As long as ever you can.

JOHN WESLEY

Let each of us please his neighbor for his good, to his edification.

ROMANS 15:2

Tact comes as much from kindness of the heart as from fineness of taste.

ENDYMION

Keep me, O Lord, from all pettiness.
Let me be large in thought and
word and deed.
Let me leave of self-seeking and have
done with fault-finding.
Help me put away all pretense, that
I may meet my neighbor face to
face, without self-pity and without prejudice.
May I never be hasty in my judgments,
but generous to all and in all things.
Make me grow calm, serene, and gentle.
Teach me to put into action my better
impulses and make me straightforward and unafraid.
Grant that I may realize that it is the
trifling things of life that create
differences, that in the higher
things we are all one.
And, O Lord, God, let me not forget
to be kind!

MARY STUART

Always...set a high
value on spontaneous
kindness.

SAMUEL JOHNSON

It is more blessed to

To cultivate kindness is a valuable
part of the business of life.

SAMUEL JOHNSON

Every soul that touches yours...

Be it the slightest contact...

Gets therefrom some good;

Some little grace; one kindly thought;

One aspiration yet unfelt;

One bit of courage

For the darkening sky,

One gleam of faith

To brave the thickening ills of life;

One glimpse of brighter skies...

To make this life worth while

And heaven a surer heritage.

GEORGE ELIOT

give than to receive.

ACTS 20:35

Kindness and truth will be to those who devise good.

PROVERBS 14:22

Prayer

Father God, I come to You this day with great conviction that the kindness we show to others is an accurate measure of how we are living out our Christian life. I want to be a person who others know as a kind person. I know that many who look upon my actions are seeing You for the first time. If they see in me kindness, they will know that You are kind. May I daily be aware of how I treat people. I truly want to treat others the way in which I want to be treated.

Thank You for modeling to me how to be kind. May I help pass on Your abundant kindness to others, so that they might one day know You and experience Your great love. Amen.

CHAPTER SIX

Goodness

*I know that there is nothing better for them than to rejoice
and do good in one's lifetime...it is the gift of God.*

ECCLESIASTES 3:12,13

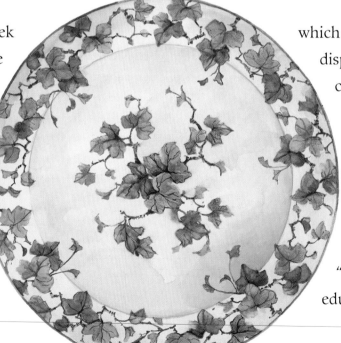

Did you know that the Greek word for "good" appears more than one hundred times in the New Testament? The translations of the word vary to include such meanings as genuine, honorable, healthy, generous, dependable, and honest. Goodness involves habitual actions which reflect a person's inward disposition. (This includes the concept of helping but, interestingly enough, can also include rebuking, correcting, and discipline.) Long before the present-day teaching of the concept of "excellence" in business, education, or church work,

Paul taught this virtuous concept called "goodness" to the early Church.

As maturing Christians, we are to grow into people of goodness. Each day we have the opportunity to show this fruit at work in our lives. The first step is to become aware of those around us who need a touch of goodness. Much as we'd like to, we can't show goodness to the whole world. However, we certainly can touch those with whom we have daily contact—our spouse, our children, our extended family, our neighbors, our coworkers. The world is so hungry to have goodness come its way. It takes so little effort to have a positive effect on those you know. And it's so easy to become known as a person who exhibits goodness in her life. Because goodness is love in action, it is easy to touch a longing and hungry world that desperately seeks people who give of themselves to enrich the lives of others. Through your actions, you can proclaim God's wonderful nature. He is good!

We know that God causes all things to work together for good to those who love God, to those who are called according to His purpose.
ROMANS 8:28

Goodness consists not in the outward things we do, but in the inward thing we are.

EDWIN HUBBELL CHAPIN

Let Thy godly ones

Real goodness does not attach itself merely to this life—it points to another world.

DANIEL WEBSTER

Enrich someone's life today with a warm word of praise. Both of you will be better for it.

AUTHOR UNKNOWN

Goodness is love in action, love with its hand at the plough, love with the burden on its back. It is love carrying medicine to the sick and food to the famished. It is love reading the Bible to the blind and explaining the gospel to the felon in his cell. It is love at the Sunday-class or in the ragged-school. It is love at the hovel-door or sailing far away in the missionary ship. But, whatever task it undertakes, it is still the same— love following His footsteps, "who went about continually doing good!"

DR. J. HAMILTON

*Surely goodness and lovingkindness will
follow me all the days of my life, and I
will dwell in the house of the Lord forever.*
PSALM 23:6

The most acceptable service
of God is doing good to man.
BENJAMIN FRANKLIN

rejoice in what is good

2 CHRONICLES 6:41

We ought to do good to others as simply and naturally as a
horse runs, or a bee makes honey, or a vine bears grapes season
after season without thinking of the grapes it has borne.

MARCUS AURELIUS

*Every good thing bestowed and every
perfect gift is from above, coming down
from the Father of lights, with whom there
is no variation, or shifting shadow.*

JAMES 1:17

43

Love, sweetness, goodness,
in her person shined.
JOHN MILTON

There is an idea
abroad among moral
people that they
should make their
neighbors good. One
person I have to make
good: myself.
ROBERT LOUIS
STEVENSON

O that men would therefore
praise the LORD for his
goodness: and declare the
wonders that he doeth for the
children of men! For he satisfieth
the empty soul: and filleth the
hungry soul with goodness.
THE BOOK OF COMMON PRAYER

Goodness is

There will be...glory and honor and peace to every man who does good.
ROMANS 2:10

If I can right a human wrong,
If I can help to make one strong,
If I can cheer with smile, or song,
Lord, show me how.
GRENVILLE KLEISER

All that is good, all that is true, all that is beautiful, all that is beneficent, be it great or small, be it perfect or fragmentary, natural as well as supernatural, moral as well as material, comes from God.
JOHN H. NEWMAN

Cling to what is good.
ROMANS 12:9

Prayer

love in action.
JAMES HAMILTON

Almighty God, the fountain of all goodness.
THE BOOK OF COMMON PRAYER

Father God, as I have learned about Your goodness, I have realized that I cannot love others until I open my heart and love You first. Love to others is my response to them as Your love has been made manifest in me. May the goodness I show to others be a reflection of how much I love You! I want the world to see You when they see the good that I do. Regardless of what I might do to ease the pain and troubles of others, I do want You to receive all of the glory. For without You, I would not be able to do the good works that You enable me to accomplish. Please remind me that all of my actions and all of my words help show Your love to a hurting world. Amen.

CHAPTER SEVEN

Faithfulness

A faithful man will abound with blessings.

PROVERBS 28:20

In our lives, we are repeatedly challenged to understand what it means to be faithful. We know we're supposed to be dedicated and committed, but when we see waverings of faithfulness in the lives of those around us, how can we ensure that we still remember what it means to have this virtue? The first thing we must do is look at our actions. When we exhibit the fruit of faithfulness, we show up on time, finish the job, are there when we need to be, and do what we say we are going to do. One of our family's favorite mottoes is: "Just do what you say you are going to do!" Can you imagine what living

out this motto would do on the job, with your spouse and children, at your church, and especially in your own life? The results would be amazing!

A successful life is based on trust and faith. Throughout the Old Testament we read of God's faithfulness to the people of Israel. No matter how much the Israelites complained about their situation, He remained faithful to His chosen people. He wanted the best for them. In the New Testament, Jesus reflects the same loyalty to His heavenly Father. He always sought God's will. Jesus' faithfulness to the Father took Him all the way to the cross so that our sins could be eternally covered. I am so glad He was faithful! Even though people today adjust their actions based on our culture's changing interpretations of faithfulness, the absolutes of Scripture make it very clear what it means for a Christian to be faithful. Someday we will stand before God and He will welcome us into heaven by saying, "Come in! Well done, good and faithful servant!" Our faithfulness is definitely worth something to our Father!

And the LORD will repay each man for his righteousness and his faithfulness.
1 SAMUEL 26:23

Reverent fear of God is the key to faithfulness in any situation.

ALAN REDPATH

He who is faithful in a very

O love the LORD, all you His godly ones! The Lord preserves the faithful.

PSALM 31:23

Many fill their life with regrets for being confined to such a narrow sphere of usefulness. If they only were in the ministerial office, or had millions of money, they would do so and so; but what can an ordinary laborer, a poor Sunday-school teacher, accomplish? Friend, be content to serve God where he has placed you; for there precisely can you accomplish the most. It is better to make the best of what you have, than to fret and pout for what you have not. The man with one talent is never accountable for five; but, for his one, he must give as strict an account as the other for his five. It may require more humility to husband one talent than five, and, so far as the improvement or misimprovement of either is concerned, they are both equally important in the sight of God. The king's million and the widow's mite are worth the same with the Eternal.

AUTHOR UNKNOWN

48

Let love and faithfulness never leave you; bind them around your neck, write them on the tablet of your heart.
PROVERBS 3:3

We must do our business faithfully, without trouble or disquiet, recalling our mind to God mildly, and with tranquility, as often as we find it wandering from him.
BROTHER LAWRENCE

little thing is faithful also in much.
LUKE 16:10

A little thing is a little thing, but faithfulness in a little thing becomes a great thing.
PLATO

One thing you can give and still keep is your word.
AUTHOR UNKNOWN

49

I have chosen the faithful way; I have placed Thine ordinances before me.

PSALM 119:30

If a man is called to be a street sweeper, he should sweep streets even as Michelangelo painted or Beethoven composed music or Shakespeare wrote poetry. He should sweep streets so well that all the hosts of heaven and earth will pause to say, "Here lived a great street sweeper who did his job well."

MARTIN LUTHER KING, JR.

A faithful friend is an

FRENCH PROVERB

All the paths of the LORD are lovingkindness and truth to those who keep His covenant and His testimonies.

PSALM 25:10

Mly eyes shall be upon the faithful of the land, that they may dwell with me.

PSALM 101:6

*This is a wise, sane Christian faith: that
a man commit himself, his life and
his hopes to God; that God undertakes the
special protection of that man; that therefore
that man ought not to be afraid of anything!*
GEORGE MACDONALD

image of God.

Prayer

Father God, I so want those around me to know that I am Your faithful follower and a faithful friend. I want to be dependable, accountable, on time, never breaking a worthy commitment, reliable, loyal, and trustworthy. I want to be counted on by others to come through for them when I'm needed. You are my model as I try to live out my life to be like You. All throughout Scripture You are pictured as Someone who is faithful, Someone who we as believers can trust. You, too, are always dependable, One who is always there when I need You. You have said that we as stewards are to be found faithful (1 Corinthians 4:2). Thank You, God, for showing me how to be faithful in all that I do. Amen.

CHAPTER EIGHT

Gentleness

I...entreat you to walk in a manner worthy of the calling with which you have been called,
with all humility and gentleness, with patience, showing forbearance to one another in love.

EPHESIANS 4:1,2

When I look at the gifts of power and strength, I'm always amazed when I see gentleness exhibited along with these qualities of might. Gentleness is a virtue that brings to mind sensitivity, a soft touch, or a very light hug. When I see a 300-pound NFL lineman interviewed on television, I'm surprised to discover that many of these huge men have a tenderness to their personality and are dedicated Christians, loving husbands, and affectionate dads. The world often equates being gentle with being a

52

coward and an easy pushover, but we know that is not the case. Gentleness takes uncommon strength!

A caring man helps an elderly person across the street. A little girl holds a china cup delicately so it won't slip and fall to the floor. A mother animal carries her young tenderly in her mouth. A friend rubs your back when it is stiff and aching. We certainly recognize gentleness when we see it! As followers of Jesus, our job is to transfer and apply this fruit of the Spirit into Christian action. In the New Testament, gentleness means submissiveness to the will of God as reflected in the words of Jesus: "Take My yoke upon you, and learn from Me, for I am gentle and humble in heart; and you shall find rest for your souls" (Matthew 11:29). To attain gentleness, our natural earthly desires need to come under the submission of God's will. We will become all that God wants us to become when we reflect a spirit of gentleness in our Christian walk.

The right kind of toughness—strength of character—ought to mark the man of today...but not only that. Tenderness—gentleness—is equally important. God considers it so important he places it on the list of nine qualities he feels should mark the life of his children...Our goal is balance...always balance. Not either-or, but both-and. Not just tough. That alone makes a man cold, distant, intolerant, unbearable. But tough and tender...gentle, thoughtful, teachable, considerate.

CHARLES SWINDOLL

Gentleness is love in society...It is that cordiality of aspect and that soul of speech, which assure that kind and earnest hearts may still be met with here below. It is that quiet influence, which, like the scented flame of an alabaster lamp, fills many a home with light and warmth and fragrance altogether. It is the carpet, soft and deep, which, whilst it diffuses a look of ample comfort, deadens many a creaking sound. It is the curtain, which from many a beloved form wards off at once the summer's glow and the winter's wind. It is the pillow on which sickness lays its head and forgets half its misery, and to which death comes in a balmier dream. It is considerateness. It is tenderness of feeling. It is warmth of affection. It is promptitude of sympathy. It is love in all its depths and all its delicacy. It is every thing included in that matchless grace, the gentleness of Christ.

DR. J. HAMILTON

Thy gentleness

Beautiful thoughts hardly bring us to God until they are acted upon. No one can have a true idea of right until he does it.

WILLIAM R. INGE

Blessed are the gentle, for they shall inherit the earth.

MATTHEW 5:5

No one knows like a woman how to say things which are at once gentle and deep.

VICTOR HUGO

makes me great.

PSALM 18:35

Life is an exciting business and most exciting when it is lived for others.

HELEN KELLER

A Christian is God Almighty's gentleman. The real gentleman should be gentle in every thing; at least in every thing that depends on himself-in carriage, temper, constructions, aims, desires. He ought, therefore, to be mild, calm, quiet, even, temperate; not hasty in judgment, not exorbitant in ambition, not overbearing, not proud, not rapacious, not oppressive: for these things are contrary to gentleness.

HARE

A gentleman saw a blind woman standing on a busy corner waiting for someone to help her cross the intersection. He stepped up to her and asked, "May I go across with you?"

AUTHOR UNKNOWN

Once upon a time when everything could talk, the Wind and the Sun fell into an argument as to which was the stronger. Finally they decided to put the matter to a test; they would see which one could make a certain man, who was walking along the road, throw off his cape. The Wind tried first. He blew and he blew. The harder and colder he blew, the tighter the traveler wrapped his cape about him. The Wind finally gave up and told the Sun to try. The Sun began to smile and as it grew warmer and warmer, the traveler was comfortable once more. But the Sun shone brighter and brighter until the man grew so hot, the sweat poured out on his face, he became weary, and seating himself on a stone, he quickly threw his cape to the ground. You see, gentleness had accomplished what force could not.

AESOP

No man or woman can really be strong, gentle, pure, and good without the world being better for it.

PHILLIP BROOKS

A gentle answer

Pursue righteousness, godliness, faith, love, perseverance and gentleness.

1 TIMOTHY 6:11

A gentleman is one who thinks more of other people's feelings than of his own rights; and more of other people's rights than of his own feelings.

MATTHEW HENRY BUCKHAM

Let not your adornment be merely external...but let it be the hidden person of the heart, with the imperishable quality of a gentle and quiet spirit, which is precious in the sight of God.

1 PETER 3:3,4

turns away wrath.

PROVERBS 15:1

Prayer

Father God, it is obvious that You cherish a gentle spirit in Your children. As I observe how the rest of the world quarrels and holds bitterness in their hearts, I know that I don't want that to be me. I give You my life so that You can use me the way You intended me to be used. When I am tempted to fall into the ways of the world, please remind me that I am Your child and that You lift up those who have gentleness in their spirits. I know that because of this spirit of gentleness, I will have less stress in my life, a more balanced lifestyle, and that I will be a more radiant person. Thank You for revealing these truths to me. Amen.

CHAPTER NINE

Self~Control

But the fruit of the Spirit is love, joy, peace, patience, kindness,
goodness, faithfulness, gentleness, and self-control.

GALATIANS 5:22,23

In Romans 7:15-25, the apostle Paul deals with a classic problem when he struggles to exercise self-control in his life: "I have the desire to do what is good, but I cannot carry it out. For what I do is not the good I want to do; no, the evil I do not want to do—this I keep on doing" (verses 18,19 NIV). Like Paul, we must often work to let the fruit of self-control grow in our lives and help us to do what is right. To do this, we need to recognize our weaknesses and vulnerabilities. And next, we must cultivate a desire for self-control in our hearts. Like an athlete who wants to attain a specific goal, we should focus upon improving our skills. With God's help and our own commitment, we can win the prize!

An important step to gaining self-control is writing down easy-to-follow steps to reach our goal. If we write these out in clear terms and give ourselves a date for completing, we will be well on our way to experiencing a fulfilling Christian walk. And the best news is that we don't have to do it all on our own! The power of the Holy Spirit will enable us to master any lack of commitment in our life. Seek out His leading, and you will be ushered into a satisfying new life of self-control.

But since we belong to the day, let us be self-controlled, putting on faith and love as a breastplate, and the hope of salvation as a helmet.
1 THESSALONIANS 5:8 NIV

Let us be alert

He must be hospitable, one who loves what is good, who is self-controlled, upright, holy and disciplined.

TITUS 1:8 NIV

Minimize friction and create harmony. You can get friction for nothing, but harmony costs courtesy and self-control.

AUTHOR UNKNOWN

Two frogs lived together in a marsh. But one hot summer the marsh dried up, and they left it to look for another place to live in, for frogs like damp places if they can get them. By and by they came to a deep well, and one of them looked down into it, and said to the other, "This looks like a nice cool place. Let us jump in and settle here." But the other, who had a wiser head on his shoulders, replied, "Not so fast, my friend. Supposing this well dried up like the marsh, how should we get out again?" Think twice before you act.

AESOP

and self~controlled.

1 THESSALONIANS 5:6 NIV

For this very reason, make every effort to add to your faith goodness; and to goodness, knowledge; and to knowledge, self-control; and to self-control, perseverance...

2 PETER 1:5,6 NIV

For God did not give us a spirit of timidity, but of power and love and discipline.

2 TIMOTHY 1:7

For the grace of God that brings salvation has appeared to all men. It teaches us to say "No" to ungodliness and worldly passions, and to live self-controlled, upright and godly lives.

TITUS 2:11,12 NIV

Self-reverence, self-knowledge, self-control, these three alone lead life to sovereign power.

TENNYSON

I do not ask for any crown
But that which all may win;
Nor try to conquer any world
Except the one within.

Be Thou my guide until I find
Led by a tender hand,
The happy kingdom in myself
And dare to take command.

LOUISA MAY ALCOTT

He who reigns within himself and rules his
passions, desires, and fears is more than a king.

MILTON

Therefore be clear
self-controlled so that

1 PETER 4:7 NIV

My God, give me neither poverty nor riches,

but whatsoever it may be Thy will to

give, give me with it a heart that knows

humbly to acquiesce in what is Thy will.

FRANCOIS DE LA ROCHEFOUCAULD

minded and

you can pray.

Prayer

Father God, we live in a day where people want to be in control, and I certainly want to have control of myself, but only under Your power. I realize that it takes a great amount of discipline to have You come into my life and direct me as You would have me go. Yet this is the way I desire to live. I thank You for being a patient God, One who walks beside me as I take little baby steps in my growth toward self-control. Each day I give my life to You. May You teach me as You see fit. When I feel stretched, stressed, and wanting control of my own life, may I be reminded that You are the one who gives me control of myself. Amen.

Beautiful Fruit

Jesus said, "By this is My Father glorified, that you bear much fruit, and so prove to be My disciples" (John 15:8). The abundance of our hearts that is the fruit of the Spirit glorifies God, and by it we demonstrate to the world around us that we are His followers. But we don't have to bear this fruit all on our own. It is only because of His indwelling presence that we can be people of love, joy, peace, patience, kindness, goodness, gentleness, and self-control. As the Holy Spirit pours out His love and grace within us, let us be devoted to producing beautiful fruit that will bless our lives and the lives we touch.